GRIEF

God's Help in Times of Sorrow

9 STUDIES FOR INDIVIDUALS OR GROUPS

Cathy Gardner Maddams & Jim Reapsome

With Notes for Leaders

IVP Connect

An imprint of InterVarsity Press
Downers Grove, Illinois

InterVarsity Press
P.O. Box 1400, Downers Grove, IL 60515-1426
World Wide Web: www.ivpress.com
E-mail: email@ivpress.com

InterVarsity Press® is the book-publishing division of InterVarsity Christian Fellowship/USA®, a movement of students and faculty active on campus at hundreds of universities, colleges and schools of nursing in the United States of America, and a member movement of the International Fellowship of Evangelical Students. For information about local and regional activities, write Public Relations Dept., InterVarsity Christian Fellowship/USA, 6400 Schroeder Rd., P.O. Box 7895, Madison, WI 53707-7895, or visit the IVCF website at <www.intervarsity.org>.

LifeGuide® is a registered trademark of InterVarsity Christian Fellowship.

All Scripture quotations, unless otherwise indicated, are taken from the Holy Bible, New International Version®. NIV®. Copyright ©1973, 1978, 1984 by International Bible Society. Used by permission of Zondervan Publishing House. All rights reserved.

Cover images: stormy sky: © Leonard/depositphotos.com
dry ground and lightning: © Clint Spencer/iStockphoto

ISBN 978-0-8308-3144-9

Printed in the United States of America ∞

 InterVarsity Press is committed to protecting the environment and to the responsible use of natural resources. As a member of Green Press Initiative we use recycled paper whenever possible. To learn more about the Green Press Initiative, visit http://www.greenpressinitiative.org

P	20	19	18	17	16	15	14	13	12	11	10	9	8	7	6	5	4	3	2	1
Y	28	27	26	25	24	23	22	21	20	19	18	17	16	15	14	13	12			

Contents

Getting the Most Out of *Grief*

When dealing with a painful loss, we often ask ourselves questions such as, *What am I going to do with my life? How will I get through each day? What if I never stop crying? Why did God let this happen?* Such fears and thoughts are very real. The two of us have experienced them in our own lives from the losses of spouses and children and have walked with others through these questions in different pastoral and healing ministries. The journey of healing is a long one that requires time, patience and loving support.

God understands your pain. He is there to give you the courage and strength to move forward. Turning to the Bible as a source of wisdom can help you through this difficult time, as the Bible offers profound insights into people's interactions with God in many difficult situations, including loss. The book of Psalms, in particular, gives us a picture of real struggles and of God's help in lifting us from our pain.

This LifeGuide will help you in the difficult journey of grieving a loss, whether it's the loss of a loved one, a marriage, a job or a home. Each study is dedicated to an emotion common to the grieving process: denial, fear, anger, guilt, sadness, hope, faith, acceptance and praise. The psalm for each study deals with the same emotion and helps us understand God's role and power in our healing. Through discussion and personal reflection we can better understand these stages of grieving and apply the practical suggestions offered.

While individuals can certainly use this guide on their own, small groups will find this to be a very meaningful study in both helping group members with their losses and equipping all members to better empathize with and understand the grieving process, as well as assist with healing. *Grief* can also be used as the basis for a grief support group led by a facilitator. The appendix at the end of the guide offers many excellent suggestions and tools for starting and conducting such a group. In addition, the leader's notes will be helpful for both small group leaders and grief group facilitators, as they provide step-by-step guidance of the discussions and important background information to support the lessons. Both of these resources will deepen and enhance the effectiveness of the study, and guide leaders in creating the safe, sensitive and confidential environment that is essential to the group's success and to each person's comfort and healing.

Group participation is a valued part of each session. The discussion questions use an inductive approach, which encourages self-discovery and honors the uniqueness of each person. Because sharing is such an important part of a grief support group, in particular, but also of small group Bible studies, we recommend that the time allotted to each lesson be extended (as agreed upon by the group) to one-and-a-half or two hours.

One of the main advantages of a Bible-based study on grief is that we receive assurance that we are not alone in our sorrow; we can help one another and see in new ways that God truly cares for us and understands our pain. Jesus himself dealt with loss and disappointment, as seen in the story about the death of Lazarus. The Bible tells us that "Jesus wept" (John 11:35) when he reached the tomb of his friend. But the story ends with great hope. And Jesus did say, "Blessed are those who mourn, for they will be comforted" (Matthew 5:4). He validated his promise because he was "a man of sorrows, acquainted with deepest grief" (Isaiah 53:3 NLT).

No matter where you are in your faith journey, if you are experiencing the loss of a spouse or child, a divorce, or the loss of your job or home, this LifeGuide can offer encouragement and understanding. By facing your grief and reaching out for help, you can receive comfort and hope.

Suggestions for Individual Study

1. As you begin each study, pray that God will speak to you through his Word.

2. Read the introduction to the study and respond to the personal reflection question or exercise. This is designed to help you focus on God and on the theme of the study.

3. Each study deals with a particular passage so that you can delve into the author's meaning in that context. Read and reread the passage to be studied. The questions are written using the language of the New International Version, so you may wish to use that version of the Bible. The New Revised Standard Version is also recommended.

4. This is an inductive Bible study, designed to help you discover for yourself what Scripture is saying. The study includes three types of questions. *Observation* questions ask about the basic facts: who, what, when, where and how. *Interpretation* questions delve into the meaning of the passage. *Application* questions help you discover the implications of the text for growing in Christ. These three keys unlock the treasures of Scripture.

Write your answers to the questions in the spaces provided or in a personal journal. Writing can bring clarity and deeper understanding of yourself and of God's Word.

5. It might be good to have a Bible dictionary handy. Use it to look up any unfamiliar words, names or places.

6. Use the prayer suggestion to guide you in thanking God for what you have learned and to pray about the applications that have come to mind.

7. You may want to go on to the suggestion under "Now or Later," or you may want to use that idea for your next study.

Suggestions for Members of a Group Study

1. Come to the study prepared. Follow the suggestions for individual study mentioned above. You will find that careful preparation will greatly enrich your time spent in group discussion.

2. Be willing to participate in the discussion. The leader of your group will not be lecturing. Instead, he or she will be encouraging the members of the group to discuss what they have learned. The leader will be asking the questions that are found in this guide.

3. Stick to the topic being discussed. Your answers should be based on the verses which are the focus of the discussion and not on outside authorities such as commentaries or speakers. These studies focus on a particular passage of Scripture. Only rarely should you refer to other portions of the Bible. This allows for everyone to participate in in-depth study on equal ground.

4. Be sensitive to the other members of the group. Listen attentively when they describe what they have learned. You may be surprised by their insights! Each question assumes a variety of answers. Many questions do not have "right" answers, particularly questions that aim at meaning or application. Instead the questions push us to explore the passage more thoroughly.

When possible, link what you say to the comments of others. Also, be affirming whenever you can. This will encourage some of the more hesitant members of the group to participate.

5. Be careful not to dominate the discussion. We are sometimes so eager to express our thoughts that we leave too little opportunity for others to respond. By all means participate! But allow others to also.

6. Expect God to teach you through the passage being discussed and through the other members of the group. Pray that you will have an enjoyable and profitable time together, but also that as a result of the study you will find ways that you can take action individually and/or as a group.

7. Remember that anything said in the group is considered confidential and should not be discussed outside the group unless specific permission is given to do so.

8. If you are the group leader, you will find additional suggestions at the back of the guide.

1

Denial

Denial is often one of the first emotions experienced in the grieving process. It's very natural to question or reject the reality of our loss. Our world has drastically changed, creating fears and worries. What was normal is no longer the same. This shakes our feelings of comfort and security. We might be tormented by thoughts like, *This can't be true. Why is this happening to me?* We also might become consumed by work or other activities to avoid facing or talking about our loss. Photographs and memories might be too painful to revisit. These are normal reactions and are part of grieving. As we face our grief, the pain and emptiness will diminish with time.

GROUP DISCUSSION. Share about your loss and how it is affecting you. What are you finding hardest to accept?

PERSONAL REFLECTION. Reflect on the value of giving yourself permission to grieve and of then facing your grief. What particular thoughts and images come to mind? Write them down or take them to God in prayer.

Like many of the Psalms, Psalm 46 was once used as part of the Jewish temple worship in Jerusalem. No author claimed it, and it was not linked to a specific event in Israel's history, but it stands as a song of worship in praise of God's love, even when in a life-threatening situation. *Read Psalm 46.*

1. How does the psalmist picture God?

2. How can God be our refuge and strength?

our ever-present help?

3. In what ways do the feelings you have about your loss relate to the scary or tragic circumstances mentioned by the psalmist?

4. Complete this sentence: "I will not fear, though . . ."

5. What does the river represent?

Why will the "city of God" not fall (vv. 4-5)?

6. What "streams" do you have to draw on as you face your loss?

7. What difference does it make that the Lord Almighty is with us (vv. 5-7, 11)?

8. What does the fortress metaphor (vv. 7, 11) tell us about God's role in our grief and loss?

9. How could obedience to the command "Be still, and know that I am God" (v. 10) provide strength when we're tempted to run from our pain?

10. What one thing (a thought, feeling or new idea) would you like to take from your experience of this study?

11. What one thing (a thought, feeling or old idea) would you like to leave behind?

Ask God to strengthen and embolden you to face the painful reality of your loss, trusting him for wholeness and healing.

Now or Later

Give yourself permission to do something nice for yourself—something that would make you feel better. For example, go to an uplifting movie or a ball game, go out to lunch or dinner with a friend, get a massage, return to a hobby, and so on. Afterward, journal or talk to God about what you did. How did it feel while you were doing it? How do you feel now? What about the activity you chose brought comfort? What about it was hard?

2

Fear

Psalm 62

Grief deeply affects our lives, to the point where there is often no sense of normal. So we might, for example, be unable to concentrate or to remember even the simplest of things. The challenge of new responsibilities might be overwhelming. We may pull away from friends because they "just don't understand," or we may need constant companionship. Home and even church may hold painful memories. We might lose motivation to go to work, eat, exercise or do anything positive for ourselves. All of these factors contribute to a state of uncertainty and anxiety. Fear is therefore natural when grieving a loss.

GROUP DISCUSSION. In what ways do you find yourself indentifying with the circumstances above? How do these examples relate to any anxieties or fears you might have?

PERSONAL REFLECTION. What are your deepest fears right now? Write them down and then incorporate them into a prayer to God.

David reigned as Israel's king for forty years. He brought unity and prosperity to his country following King Saul's disastrous reign, yet he also faced serious threats to his throne and life—including Saul's murderous pursuit of him before he was king and then open rebellion by one of his sons. Many of the psalms he wrote reveal some of his hardest struggles and show how his faith in God sustained him. *Read Psalm 62.*

1. With what facts about God does David arm himself (vv. 1-2, 5-8, 11-12)?

2. What main picture of God emerges?

3. What do you think this picture did for David?

4. Use your own metaphors to complete this sentence: "God is my . . ."

How can your word pictures of God help you and strengthen you?

5. According to this psalm, what kind of rest does God provide?

How does God make "soul rest" available?

---

6. Twice David affirms that he will not be shaken (vv. 2, 6)—in other words, that he will not be troubled or upset or, as one translation puts it, "tense with fear" (LB)—even while facing threats to his life and his throne. What circumstances cause you to become "tense with fear"? Why?

---

7. What does David exhort his people to do (v. 8)?

---

8. How does trust diminish fear?

---

9. To what does David look for satisfaction instead of position and wealth (vv. 9-12)?

To what are you tempted to look for comfort or satisfaction?

10. How do God's strength and love help us to deal with our fears and anxieties?

Thank God for all that you have learned about him. Pray that you will find in God the strength, courage and faith to overcome your fears.

Now or Later

Express an overwhelming fear to a trusted person. Notice if the fear has less control over you after you express it. Be sure to use God's gift of prayer. For example, breathe a simple request to God. Imagine that God is asking you what you want or need. The breath prayer is your answer to him. It may be one word such as *peace, wisdom* or *help,* or it may be several words such as "Give me strength." You could also write a brief prayer in your journal. In addition, it might be helpful to revisit Psalm 46 from study one and pray it back to God.

3

Anger

Anger is an emotion that can be extremely difficult to express or even acknowledge, especially in a society like ours where the expression of anger is discouraged. However, anger is a normal and predictable component of grieving. It indicates that we have been deeply hurt by our circumstances. We're frustrated by what has happened and how profoundly our life has been changed.

At its core, anger is energy we can either suppress or invest. If we bottle our anger inside, or if it is medicated by drugs or alcohol, we could find ourselves in a cycle of self-destruction, including physical and emotional illness, anxiety and depression.

The apostle Paul said, "Be angry and do not sin" (Ephesians 4:26 ESV). Anger is part of God's design for us; we can embrace it by choosing to invest its energy and learning how to express it in nonthreatening, unharmful ways.

GROUP DISCUSSION. In what ways is anger affecting you in your grieving? How have you tried to deal with it?

PERSONAL REFLECTION. How has anger affected your body in the past? your thinking? your reactions? What would it look like for you to "invest" your anger in more positive outlets? Ask God for wisdom and understanding.

This intensely personal psalm reveals the deep distress of the psalmist. His desperate condition could have been caused by a tragedy in his life or by some natural disaster. Although we cannot link it to a specific event, such disasters were not uncommon in Israel's history. The writer took his nation's troubles to heart and his anxieties to God, eventually coming to renewed faith, courage and hope. *Read Psalm 77.*

1. If you were directing a one-act play based on this psalm, what instructions would you give the actor for this monologue?

2. What questions does the psalmist have about God (vv. 7-9)?

3. Why do you think voicing the depth of his anguish to God is important for the psalmist?

4. Which of his feelings can you best relate to?

5. What is the greatest cause of your frustration and anger right now? Why?

6. How do you express your anger to God?

7. What does the psalmist decide to do with his anger (vv. 10-12)?

8. What is the value of the psalmist's new outlook on his problem?

9. Where are you in your understanding of and relation to God?

10. What can you learn from the psalmist about dealing with your anger in relationship with God?

11. What facts about God are true, regardless of how we feel?

12. The psalmist reflects on God's deliverance from bondage in Egypt (vv. 13-20). Of what value could it be to you in the midst of your loss to recall God's provisions for you and faithfulness to you in the past?

Ask God to help you express your anger and frustration to him and then use that energy in healthy ways, like the psalmist did.

Now or Later

Choose a specific way to express your anger. For example, you could write about it, talk with God honestly about how you feel, find release in exercise, keep a journal, record yourself talking or share your feelings with someone you trust.

Then reflect on a time when you believe God answered a prayer in your life. Like the psalmist, write down the details of that experience and use that memory to offer thanks to God and strengthen your trust in him.

4

Guilt

Although intense feelings of anger and guilt are somewhat similar in terms of the harm they can cause, they also differ substantially. Most anger is directed at someone else; we fasten the blame or responsibility on others. With guilt, however, we blame ourselves for something we did or thought, or for something we did not do. In small doses, guilt keeps us honest and can be productive. But if our guilt is magnified and misdirected, it can become overwhelming and cause great suffering. Even when our guilt is not necessarily rational (which is often the case with grief), the feelings are very real and must be acknowledged.

GROUP DISCUSSION. What guilt feelings do you carry regarding your loss? Why?

PERSONAL REFLECTION. How can carrying your guilt be harmful to you? How could releasing your guilt be beneficial? Journal in detail about the guilt you feel.

Psalm 32, another psalm of David, is based on repentance. David had suffered because of unconfessed sin, but after his confession he found God's assurance of forgiveness. The psalm became part of temple worship as a song of thanksgiving. Some churches use it during their Ash Wednesday service. *Read Psalm 32.*

1. Confronted by his sin, what choices did David have (see vv. 3-4 and v. 5)?

2. Put in your own words how David's guilt affected him.

Of what ultimate value were his feelings of guilt?

3. Why did he confess to God?

4. How did God respond to David's confession (v. 5)?

5. How do you think God will respond to you if you confess to him the guilt you're feeling?

Why do you think this?

6. What advice does David give as a result of God's response to his confession (vv. 6, 9, 11)?

7. What does he promise God will do (vv. 7, 8, 10)?

8. Retrace the steps of David's spiritual journey from verses 3-4 to verse 11. How does his experience help you in your prayers?

in taking steps toward healing?

9. Why is it sometimes hard to forgive ourselves?

10. Where do you see yourself in this psalm?

Ask God to free you from your feelings of guilt related to your loss. Ask him for a growing sense of confidence in his love and protection as you anticipate a time of relief and even rejoicing.

Now or Later

Several things can be done to heal guilt feelings. If you have done something to someone and feel guilty about it, write to this person and express your regrets. Ask for forgiveness. If the person has died, write the letter and then write down what this person would say back to you. Consider sharing every detail about your guilt with God and humbly ask for forgiveness. Then honor God by accepting his forgiveness.

5

Sadness

Sadness is one of the most difficult emotions to deal with after a painful loss or life change. Life seems to continue around you, but you're not able to jump back into your life as you see others doing. Grief and loss have stolen any sense of normalcy. This reality can lead to resentment, isolation, loneliness and depression. You may find it very uncomfortable to talk about what has happened and the consequent sadness. Friends may shy away from the subject because they don't know what to say and don't want to bring up things that would make you even sadder. Moreover, being with friends can make the pain of the loss more acute, because things aren't the same anymore. In moments and days when the sadness lifts, you might feel guilty about wanting to have fun. All of these emotions are commonly felt when experiencing loss.

GROUP DISCUSSION. What feelings related to sadness have been the hardest for you to deal with? When do you most feel those emotions, and what intensifies them?

PERSONAL REFLECTION. Reflect on your patterns of sadness. What can you do to help yourself through the saddest times? How can you fill your loneliest moments? Pray for guidance.

King David wrote this psalm when he was in the wilderness of Maon fleeing from King Saul (1 Samuel 23:24-25). *Read Psalm 31.*

1. What pictures does David use to describe his relationship with God (vv. 1-3)?

2. What does David believe to be true of God?

3. From what feelings did David seek relief (vv. 9-13)?

What similar feelings are you experiencing, and why?

4. How did David's neighbors and friends react toward David (vv. 11-12)?

5. What different types or components of prayer do you find in this psalm?

6. In the midst of his pain, what specific help did David find in God (vv. 1-8, 14-16, 19-20, 21-24)?

_____

7. How does turning to God ease the pain of loneliness?

_____

8. What picture of God emerges from this psalm?

_____

9. How can you develop a keener sense of God's presence?

_____

10. Turning to God helps ease our loneliness. What other means besides himself has God given to help us?

_____

11. In one or two sentences, name the ways a friend has helped you in your grief.

Tell God about your sadness and loneliness and ask him to show you how to claim his love and his presence. Ask God for courage and trust to share your true feelings with friends who care and want to help. Pray as well for courage and wisdom to reach out to others in their sadness.

Now or Later

You have already taken a big step in dealing with your difficult emotions by choosing to do this study. Continue to move forward by reaching out and responding to others, as they may not know how or when to offer their support. If someone asks, "How can I help?" or "What do you need?" try to offer a suggestion (like asking them to pray for you). Look for ways in which you can be of help to others as well.

In addition, give yourself permission to laugh and find moments of fun, and then appreciate the lightness and improved well-being you might feel. Plan to take specific steps to ease your sadness and your feelings of isolation. For example, go back to activities you enjoy such as a favorite hobby, your preferred type of physical exercise, outings with others, or the peacefulness of quiet reflection and journaling.

Take time to thank God in prayer or in a letter for these positive steps toward healing and for his ever-present love. Be gentle with yourself. Healing takes time.

6

Hope

At first glance, hope seems to be far beyond the realm of possibility for people struggling with grief. How do we begin to reconstruct our lives so that we can have a hopeful future? A powerful first step in our healing is to more consciously take notice of things outside ourselves that give us purpose and meaning. For example, we can find hope in little things like the beauty of a sunset, the color of a butterfly, the kindness of a friend or a baby's smile. When the future seems unsure, or even threatening, we have strong reasons to seek hope through God's help and his everlasting love. Reading the Bible, meditation and prayer are most helpful.

GROUP DISCUSSION. What things in life give you a sense of hope and touch you in a meaningful way? What brings purpose to your life?

PERSONAL REFLECTION. What reasons do you have to seek hope through God's ever-present help and love? Write down a few of these reasons. As you read the Bible, meditate and pray, ask yourself, "What things bring meaning to my life? What is the value of doing something for someone else?"

In Hebrew, Psalm 33 is not ascribed to an author, but the Greek version ascribes it to David. It may commemorate some national deliverance of Israel, but it's impossible to fix it to a specific occasion. What is clear, however, is that it's a psalm of praise and hope that edifies the Lord as Creator and Deliverer. *Read Psalm 33.*

1. What commands does the psalmist give (vv. 1-3)?

2. Why does he give these particular commands (vv. 4-5)?

3. What captures the psalmist's attention in verses 6-9?

Of what value is that in the midst of our grief?

4. What hope does he find in God's control of the nations (vv. 10-12)?

5. What perspectives do you gain from the psalmist on divine power and human strength (vv. 13-17)?

6. From the promises of God mentioned in this psalm, what gives you hope (vv. 18-19)?

How does that give you hope?

7. Review the psalmist's word pictures of God. How would you summarize his description? What understanding does he have of who God is?

8. Define hope according to this psalm.

9. How does the psalmist's outlook differ from the popular notion of hope (or "vain hope," v. 17)?

10. What gives you courage and hope to move on with your life?

11. How can you, like the psalmist, focus your attention this week on God's greatness?

Pray for God to lift your burden of despair and fill you with hope. Thank him for something in your life that brings you encouragement and purpose.

Now or Later

As you review this study, think about what steps you can take to build your hope. For example, what specific things bring you courage, hope and meaning? Write down your thoughts and discuss them with someone else. In addition, practice looking at the positives in your life (your family and friends, for example) and at God's everlasting love. Be careful to observe and record positive values and outcomes that emerge from this way of thinking. Also look for ways to encourage someone else and reflect on how this gives you hope.

7

Faith

According to *Merriam-Webster's Collegiate Dictionary,* faith is having a firm belief in something for which there is no proof. In other words, faith is based on trust. With the uncertainties that accompany grief, it is natural to question our belief system and to perhaps doubt God's existence. What once seemed like dependable truth is now not so certain. On the other hand, grief can draw us to deeper faith in God. Turning to him for comfort brings strength and guidance. Healing comes from building assurance that the future holds hope, love and new possibilities. Even during grief, when the future seems especially uncertain, faith allows us to move ahead.

GROUP DISCUSSION. What acceptable definitions of faith have you found? Where are you in your faith journey with God?

PERSONAL REFLECTION. What issues might be blocking your faith right now?

Psalm 100 was used in Jewish temple worship in connection with sacrifices of thanksgiving. It's part of a series of psalms that begins with Psalm 95, which is a call for Israel to worship God, and then fittingly climaxes with this psalm, exhorting the whole earth to acknowledge Jehovah as the only true God. *Read Psalm 100.*

1. Gladness and joy are hallmarks of faith (100:1-2). How does the psalmist's description of gladness and joy differ from a more secular understanding?

2. What aspects of faith emerge from this psalm?

3. When your soul feels dry and barren, how do you respond to God's desire for your worship?

4. How does the psalmist define and describe the relationship between the Lord and his people (100:3)?

What is significant about his description?

5. *Read John 10:1-5.* How was this metaphor from Psalm 100:3 further developed by Jesus to encourage people to have faith in him?

6. When have you experienced the truths of Psalm 100:3 and John 10:1-5 in your own life?

7. The psalmist tells us to "shout," "worship," "come," "know," "enter," "give thanks" and "praise." Why was he so eager to put such a positive spin on his life of faith?

8. Why is public praise and worship so important (100:4)?

9. What reasons does the psalmist give for trusting God (100:5)?

How can we come to know and trust these same truths about God?

10. In what ways can your faith in God help to lift you out of your grief?

If your faith feels weak at this time in your life, tell God in prayer. Ask him to reassure you of his love so that you can trust him for your future.

Now or Later

Make a list of the things that you hold to be true and describe what you believe about God and your faith. Then write down your ideas for how to build your faith. For example, you could follow a regular, daily, Bible-reading plan. Or you might keep a prayer journal and record God's answers to your prayers. Participating in worship and small fellowship groups can also help build your faith. Talk to people of faith and ask them to share about their own faith-building techniques and tell their faith journey. Then finish this sentence: "I feel more trusting about my future because . . ."

8

Acceptance

A significant step in the healing process occurs when we begin emotionally and intellectually to accept the fact that the life we once knew—our "normal" life—is not going to return. Although this is one of the hardest steps to take, it's also one of the most important, as it allows us to slowly move toward our new life. If we concentrate on building a strong foundation of support around us and trust that God will "make our steps firm," we can begin this process of moving forward.

GROUP DISCUSSION. In what ways have you begun to accept that you are building a new life?

PERSONAL REFLECTION. How are memories affecting you now? Spend some time reflecting on this statement: "You never fully recover from grieving, but the pain gradually diminishes with the help of your treasured memories."

David wrestled throughout his life with the prosperity of the wicked. In Psalm 37, however, he seems to have come to a place of acceptance: he still sees and acknowledges the difficulty of the present (that the wicked do prosper), but he's able to accept it and trust in the reality of God's eventual complete victory over evil, as well as his help for the present. *Read Psalm 37.*

1. Identify David's exhortations throughout the psalm.

What one major theme or idea best summarizes his instructions?

2. Based on this psalm, how would you describe his relationship with God?

What effect does his relationship with God have on the way he views and lives his life?

3. What kinds of thoughts, feelings and actions are the opposite of

    fretfulness:

    envy:

    trusting in God:

    delighting in God:

    committing your way to God:

    being still:

    waiting patiently for God:

4. How does David demonstrate acceptance in this psalm?

---

5. Why is it hard for us in times of grief and loss to trust God, believe in him and be patient?

---

6. Identify and put into your own words all the promises David makes to those who follow his advice and respond to God as he did.

---

7. How do these promises inspire you to accept your circumstances and grow in your faith?

---

8. Describe your mental image of someone in grief making the case to others that God is still trustworthy, as David does here. What might they say? What would their demeanor and tone of voice be like?

---

9. How could David praise God in light of the reality of his and God's enemies?

10. David's conclusion (vv. 39-40) rests on his familiar images of God as his stronghold. What images of God do you meditate on to help you accept your new different life and depend on him?

11. As a result of reading this psalm, how would you complete this sentence: "I am growing in my acceptance of . . ."?

Ask God to help you to accept your new life. Pray that you will build your trust in God so that you can rely on him through difficult times and praise him in joyful times. Thank God for his love and faithfulness.

Now or Later

Look through pictures to recall some of your most treasured memories. Write down actions you can take to honor a loved one and your past. Then take time to read slowly and thoughtfully through Psalm 37 again and ask God to reveal himself to you in your present circumstances.

9

Praise

We have been reminded by our studies from Psalms that God is always with us. We may not feel his presence in the midst of our pain, but he is there. We may lack strength to pray and to praise him, but we can let others pray for and with us. And while we may not understand why our life has changed so dramatically, we can tell ourself that God is eager to comfort us. His love is always available to us. He can sustain us and restore our lives if we place our trust in him, acknowledge his ever-present love and offer him our praise.

GROUP DISCUSSION. How can you better connect with God and receive the strength and comfort he provides? Why do you think that trust, acknowledgment and praise are so important in this process?

PERSONAL REFLECTION. In the past few weeks, how has God revealed himself to you? Through little miracles or "coincidences"? Through a conversation or a specific passage of Scripture? In some other way?

The author of Psalm 71 was apparently an old man living in exile (vv. 9, 18). His circumstances might have been similar to those of the prophet Jeremiah when he was taken captive to Egypt. In any case, the psalm is the cry of a faithful person who has experienced God's goodness in a life of many trials. It is often read today to comfort the sick. *Read Psalm 71.*

1. What does the psalmist pray for (vv. 1-4, 9, 12-13, 18)?

2. On what qualities of God does his confidence in God rest?

3. How does he portray his relationship with God?

4. How would you describe your spiritual journey? How has God factored into your life?

5. What does his hope in God do for him (v. 8)?

6. What success have you had in praising God, even when you are hurt, angry and disappointed?

7. Why was the psalmist driven to God (vv. 9-13)?

8. God's faithfulness to the psalmist inspired certain commitments. What were they (vv. 14-17)?

9. Compare the psalmist's plight with his hope and faith. What makes the difference in his outlook (vv. 20-21)?

10. Summarize the importance and practice of praise (vv. 22-24).

List everything for which the psalmist was thankful.

11. What would you include in your own psalm of praise?

Pray that you will learn to trust God in all circumstances, and to praise him even in the midst of hardships. Seek the courage and confidence to praise him before others. Offer a simple, brief prayer aloud, such as, "God, I praise you for . . ."

Now or Later

Choose a number of Bible passages to read over the next month and share them with a friend—someone who can help you be accountable to your commitment. As you read the passages each day, think about things in your life that remind you of God's care. Be alert for the little "miracles" that occur in your life and praise God as they happen. Writing them down is helpful too. Consider choosing Psalm 23, 84, 103, 139 or 145; Proverbs 3; and/or New Testament passages like John 14 and Romans 8. Or discover your own favorite passages.

Leader's Notes

MY GRACE IS SUFFICIENT FOR YOU. (2 COR 12:9)

Leading a Bible discussion can be an enjoyable and rewarding experience. But it can also be *scary*—especially if you've never done it before. If this is your feeling, you're in good company. When God asked Moses to lead the Israelites out of Egypt, he replied, "O Lord, please send someone else to do it!" (Ex 4:13). It was the same with Solomon, Jeremiah and Timothy, but God helped these people in spite of their weaknesses, and he will help you as well.

You don't need to be an expert on the Bible or a trained teacher to lead a Bible discussion. The idea behind these inductive studies is that the leader guides group members to discover for themselves what the Bible has to say. This method of learning will allow group members to remember much more of what is said than a lecture would.

These studies are designed to be led easily. As a matter of fact, the flow of questions through the passage from observation to interpretation to application is so natural that you may feel that the studies lead themselves. This study guide is also flexible. You can use it with a variety of groups—student, professional, neighborhood or church groups. There are some important facts to know about group dynamics and encouraging discussion. The suggestions listed below should enable you to effectively and enjoyably fulfill your role as leader.

Preparing for the Study

1. Ask God to help you understand and apply the passage in your own life. Unless this happens, you will not be prepared to lead others. Pray too for the various members of the group. Ask God to open your hearts to the message of his Word and motivate you to action.

2. Read the introduction to the entire guide to get an overview of the entire book and the issues which will be explored.

3. As you begin each study, read and reread the assigned Bible passage to familiarize yourself with it.

4. This study guide is based on the New International Version of the Bible. It will help you and the group if you use this translation as the basis for your study and discussion.

5. Carefully work through each question in the study. Spend time in meditation and reflection as you consider how to respond.

6. Write your thoughts and responses in the space provided in the study guide. This will help you to express your understanding of the passage clearly.

7. It might help to have a Bible dictionary handy. Use it to look up any unfamiliar words, names or places. (For additional help on how to study a passage, see chapter five of *How to Lead a LifeGuide Bible Study*, InterVarsity Press.)

8. Consider how you can apply the Scripture to your life. Remember that the group will follow your lead in responding to the studies. They will not go any deeper than you do.

9. Once you have finished your own study of the passage, familiarize yourself with the leader's notes for the study you are leading. These are designed to help you in several ways. First, they tell you the purpose the study guide author had in mind when writing the study. Take time to think through how the study questions work together to accomplish that purpose. Second, the notes provide you with additional background information or suggestions on group dynamics for various questions. This information can be useful when people have difficulty understanding or answering a question. Third, the leader's notes can alert you to potential problems you may encounter during the study.

10. If you wish to remind yourself of anything mentioned in the leader's notes, make a note to yourself below that question in the study.

Leading the Study

1. Begin the study on time. Open with prayer, asking God to help the group to understand and apply the passage.

2. Be sure that everyone in your group has a study guide. Encourage the group to prepare beforehand for each discussion by reading the introduction to the guide and by working through the questions in the study.

3. At the beginning of your first time together, explain that these studies are meant to be discussions, not lectures. Encourage the members of the group to participate. However, do not put pressure on those who may be hesitant to speak during the first few sessions. You may want to suggest the following guidelines to your group.

☐ Stick to the topic being discussed.

☐ Your responses should be based on the verses which are the focus of the discussion and not on outside authorities such as commentaries or speakers.

☐ These studies focus on a particular passage of Scripture. Only rarely should you refer to other portions of the Bible. This allows for everyone to participate in in-depth study on equal ground.

☐ Anything said in the group is considered confidential and will not be discussed outside the group unless specific permission is given to do so.

☐ We will listen attentively to each other and provide time for each person present to talk.

☐ We will pray for each other.

4. Have a group member read the introduction at the beginning of the discussion.

5. Every session begins with a group discussion question. The question or activity is meant to be used before the passage is read. The question introduces the theme of the study and encourages group members to begin to open up. Encourage as many members as possible to participate, and be ready to get the discussion going with your own response.

This section is designed to reveal where our thoughts or feelings need to be transformed by Scripture. That is why it is especially important not to read the passage before the discussion question is asked. The passage will tend to color the honest reactions people would otherwise give because they are, of course, supposed to think the way the Bible does.

You may want to supplement the group discussion question with an ice-breaker to help people to get comfortable. See the community section of *Small Group Idea Book* for more ideas.

You also might want to use the personal reflection question with your group. Either allow a time of silence for people to respond individually or discuss it together.

6. Have a group member (or members if the passage is long) read aloud the passage to be studied. Then give people several minutes to read the passage again silently so that they can take it all in.

7. Question 1 will generally be an overview question designed to briefly survey the passage. Encourage the group to look at the whole passage, but try to avoid getting sidetracked by questions or issues that will be addressed later in the study.

8. As you ask the questions, keep in mind that they are designed to be used just as they are written. You may simply read them aloud. Or you may prefer to express them in your own words.

There may be times when it is appropriate to deviate from the study guide. For example, a question may have already been answered. If so, move on to the next question. Or someone may raise an important question not covered in the guide. Take time to discuss it, but try to keep the group from going off on tangents.

9. Avoid answering your own questions. If necessary, repeat or rephrase them until they are clearly understood. Or point out something you read in the leader's notes to clarify the context or meaning. An eager group quickly becomes passive and silent if they think the leader will do most of the talking.

10. Don't be afraid of silence. People may need time to think about the question before formulating their answers.

11. Don't be content with just one answer. Ask, "What do the rest of you think?" or "Anything else?" until several people have given answers to the question.

12. Acknowledge all contributions. Try to be affirming whenever possible. Never reject an answer. If it is clearly off-base, ask, "Which verse led you to that conclusion?" or again, "What do the rest of you think?"

13. Don't expect every answer to be addressed to you, even though this will probably happen at first. As group members become more at ease, they will begin to truly interact with each other. This is one sign of healthy discussion.

14. Don't be afraid of controversy. It can be very stimulating. If you don't resolve an issue completely, don't be frustrated. Move on and keep it in mind for later. A subsequent study may solve the problem.

15. Periodically summarize what the group has said about the passage. This helps to draw together the various ideas mentioned and gives continuity to the study. But don't preach.

16. At the end of the Bible discussion you may want to allow group members a time of quiet to work on an idea under "Now or Later." Then discuss what you experienced. Or you may want to encourage group members to work on these ideas between meetings. Give an opportunity during the session for people to talk about what they are learning.

17. Conclude your time together with conversational prayer, adapting the prayer suggestion at the end of the study to your group. Ask for God's help in following through on the commitments you've made.

18. End on time.

Many more suggestions and helps are found in *How to Lead a LifeGuide Bible Study.*

Components of Small Groups

A healthy small group should do more than study the Bible. There are four components to consider as you structure your time together.

Nurture. Small groups help us to grow in our knowledge and love of God. Bible study is the key to making this happen and is the foundation of your small group.

Community. Small groups are a great place to develop deep friendships with other Christians. Allow time for informal interaction before and after each study. Plan activities and games that will help you get to know each other. Spend time having fun together going on a picnic or cooking dinner together.

Worship and prayer. Your study will be enhanced by spending time praising God together in prayer or song. Pray for each other's needs and keep track of how God is answering prayer in your group. Ask God to help you to apply what you are learning in your study.

Outreach. Reaching out to others can be a practical way of applying what you are learning, and it will keep your group from becoming self-focused. Host a series of evangelistic discussions for your friends or neighbors. Clean up the yard of an elderly friend. Serve at a soup kitchen together, or spend a day working on a Habitat house.

Many more suggestions and helps in each of these areas are found in *Small Group Idea Book*. Information on building a small group can be found in *Small Group Leaders' Handbook* and *The Big Book on Small Groups* (both from InterVarsity Press). Reading through one of these books would be worth your time.

Study 1. Denial. Psalm 46.

Purpose: To begin the steps of healing by dealing with denial and to start listening to God through this psalm.

Introduction. Open with a brief prayer. Even if your group has been together for a while, review general guidelines for the group and for the Bible study and then discuss and agree on the length of time your group meetings will run for this guide, considering the importance of having enough time for people to share. Allowing one-and-a-half to two hours per session is highly recommended. Encourage each person to participate in order to receive the most benefit from this study. You might also explain that each week there will be a theme on which the discussion and Bible study is based. The themes will help guide them through many of the emotions and experiences they may face in their grief process.

In each group meeting, we suggest doing an icebreaker after you pray (see the section "The Important First Meeting" in the appendix). We also suggest reading the opening paragraphs aloud.

Group Discussion. Allow ample time for each member to share their answer to this discussion question.

Personal Reflection. These questions are not only for people who might use this guide on their own. Group members can be strongly encouraged to reflect on the questions in the week ahead.

Question 1. Some group members may be more familiar with biblical imagery than others. Be prepared for and allow thoughtful silence. Biblical writers used everyday experiences to convey God's work in their lives. Similar images occur today in pop music, for example.

Verse 1 literally reads, "A help in distress, he [God] has let himself be found exceedingly." This was not simply the psalmist's generalization, but his report of a recent experience. Verse 2 can be taken literally or metaphorically, as a vivid sketch of utter confusion.

Question 2. These creative metaphors come from a writer who spoke from his own intimate experiences with God, not from a theological textbook. Have someone look up the word _refuge_ in the dictionary for further clarity.

Questions 3 and 4. Depending on how comfortable your group is sharing more personal answers with each other, there may be some reluctance to answer these questions, especially since it's the first study of this guide. Gently encourage members to share and reflect.

Question 5. Members may give a variety of ideas. Guide them to look at the text for their responses. The gently flowing river fertilizes the surrounding land through its channels and backwaters and thus symbolizes God's presence. Abundant irrigation was indispensable. This river is a perennial stream, not a wadi. (A wadi is a channel or watercourse that is dry except during periods of rainfall.) Compare to Isaiah 33:21 where God is compared to a mighty river. Note the contrast between the river and a raging torrent (v. 5). "The holy place" of God's dwelling "will not fall" (vv. 4-5) because it is more stable than the mountains and more secure than earthly kingdoms.

Question 6. Help the group to think of streams as sources of strength and support.

Question 8. Doubts might come into play here. Some may feel that God has hurt or disappointed them, and may therefore wonder how he could be with them in the face of grief and loss. Do not try to correct what might seem to be "wrong" answers.

Question 9. "Be still" may appear to be Pollyanna thinking, but in actuality the command takes strong action of heart and mind, not simple resignation. Being still requires the faith, courage and strength of Moses and the Israelites as they stood firm when caught between the Egyptians and the Red Sea (Ex 14:13-14). In the psalmist's immediate circumstances, it is either a command to the nations to stop fighting, or to the Israelites to reject foreign alliances.

Questions 10 and 11. Some people may not feel comfortable answering this out loud. You might invite those who don't share their answers with the group to write them down and tell them to a friend at some point in the week.

Study 2. Fear. Psalm 62.

Purpose: To understand that fears and anxiety are natural when grieving and that expressing them can help to reduce their negative impact.

Group Discussion. Feel free to rephrase the discussion question to something like, Which of these conditions have you experienced? Encourage everyone to share.

Question 2. Aim for a summary that includes all the facts to build a big-picture view of God's character.

Question 4. Some may not be familiar with the term _metaphor._ For clarification, read verse 2 together as an example of how David uses objects to describe the attributes of God.

Another way to phrase the second part of this question is "Why did you choose the specific word pictures for God that you did?" You should have some examples of your own—both metaphors and why you picked them—ready to share. For example, if one of your word pictures is "God is my anchor," you can explain to the group that you picked "anchor" because it's an image of being rooted and immovable, even during storms. Other metaphors could be a giant, 250-year-old sequoia tree, an old lighthouse or a hammock; the group will most likely come up with a range of creative metaphors. When we need these qualities in our lives, it is helpful to think of our word pictures of God, so that abstract ideas become real.

Question 5. "Find rest" (v. 5) is the psalmist's self-exhortation to maintain the calmness of verse 1 in view of his enemies' behavior (vv. 3-4). "My hope" refers to his salvation (cf. Ps 37:7). "In the first half of the psalm (vv. 1-7) the description of his plight—harassed by ruthless and treacherous enemies (vv. 3-4)—is sandwiched between a double expression of his certainty about God (vv. 1-2, 5-7). There is no need for him to keep on crying to God; he is so sure of the dependability of God that he is content silently to await God's deliverance" (F. F. Bruce, general ed., *New International Bible Commentary* [Grand Rapids: Zondervan, 1986], p. 597).

Note that "soul rest" may be a new idea to some. Give simple, practical examples of how this works for you.

Question 6. The setting of this psalm is probably the rebellion of David's son, Absalom (vv. 3-4). Unscrupulous, hypocritical enemies sought to depose David. Even some of his friends—whom he should have been able to appeal to for help—were wavering and tempted to betray him because of the power and promises of David's enemies (v. 9).

Question 8. Gently encourage people to give specific ideas, not vague generalities.

Question 9. Answers to this question could include a host of outlets: alcohol, drugs, parties, travel, sexual adventures, exotic religions, strenuous physical activity and so on.

Question 10. Some members may feel abandoned by God and therefore angry and disappointed. Seek thoughtful answers, not pat ones. Ask one or two people who are finding God's help to tell their stories.

Now or Later. Writing down thoughts and feelings can be valuable if someone feels that talking with another person about an overwhelming fear or anxiety seems too threatening. What's most important here is that people express their emotions in some way.

If you know that this will be someone's first experience of prayer, more explanation may be needed.

Study 3. Anger. Psalm 77.

Purpose: To be honest about our anger and learn from the psalmist how to experience a positive outcome from our anger.

Question 2. Encourage members to respond in their own words.

Question 3. The psalmist had to be honest with God about his feelings before he could turn to the Lord. Bottling up anger is self-defeating. Healing comes from confessing our true hurts, pain and grief to God. A fine biblical example of this principle is the experience of the prophet Habakkuk.

Question 7. The psalmist first outlines his problem (vv. 1-9). He then finds the solution by looking to God's revelation of himself in history (vv. 10-12), especially in his redemption of Israel from Egypt (vv. 13-19), and to God's guidance of his people through the wilderness (v. 20). The history of God's work is the most convincing answer to his questions, the finest elixir for his fainting spirits.

Question 9. This will be hard for some to express verbally. Don't rush in and tell them what their response is supposed to include.

Question 10. Not everyone can be expected to say something here. Explain the value of shedding negative attitudes and looking over the ideas for at least one new thing to take away from this session. Aim for specific answers, not vague generalities.

Question 11. This is the key to the psalmist's relief. "The psalmist needed no other argument. It was enough that God had revealed Himself—once and for all—on Israel's side. The beginning guaranteed the end. The dynamic landmark of the Exodus was a signpost that pointed unerringly on, an earnest of faith's fulfillment. In a sense the promised land still lay ahead, and the psalmist soldiers on in the darkness, daunted no more but with firm step and light ablaze in his heart" (*New International Bible Commentary*, p. 609).

Encourage group members to dig deeply here. You might want to have a piece of posterboard or a whiteboard available to write the facts on so people can see the list.

Question 12. The poetry here covers the gamut of Israel's story from the exodus from Egypt to the crossing of the Red Sea.

Closing Prayer. Give time for members to pray silently as they ask God to help them deal with their anger.

Now or Later. Encourage members to try one or more of the suggestions offered and notice if they feel a sense of relief or release.

Study 4. Guilt. Psalm 32.

Purpose: To understand the physical and mental harm caused by unexpressed guilt, and to acknowledge the benefits of confessing guilt (in written form, in discussion, in prayer) and then accepting forgiveness.

Question 1. This psalm is generally thought to have been composed by David after he committed adultery and murder (see 2 Sam 11). Confronted by the prophet Nathan, David confessed, "I have sinned against the LORD" (2 Sam 12:13). In the psalm, David first celebrates the blessing of forgiveness and then describes how he had suffered before he confessed to the Lord. His suffering was both emotional and physical because of God's heavy hand upon him.

Verses 3 and 4 may refer to actual physical suffering, or to the piercing pain of his conscience. Affliction often, but not always, points to sin. "My strength was sapped" (v. 4) literally means "my moisture (NEB 'sap'; i.e., 'vitality') was changed" (*New International Bible Commentary*, p. 578).

Question 2. Some may be confused by the concept that guilt feelings can be beneficial. Help them to understand that guilt can be the factor that draws us to God and motivates change and repentance.

Question 3. Briefly point out that David recognized that he had broken God's laws and therefore needed to confess to him. He was also longing for forgiveness from God, for a release from guilt and for restored intimacy in his relationship with God.

Question 5. Allow time for thoughtful personal reflection. Members may be on the way to finding release from their guilt and most likely have not yet arrived. Make clear that feelings of loss occur for many reasons. In David's case, it was because of his real, unconfessed sin. Many people in grief suffer from self-imposed, unfounded guilt.

Help those with self-imposed guilt to be aware of the false guilt they're carrying—guilt for something that was not their fault. True sin must be confessed, but self-imposed guilt is a different problem.

On the other hand, those wrestling with guilt over real sin may need to be reminded that confessing our sin and being forgiven is a life-changing experience. Finding release is often a process, however, and takes time. There must be a God-awareness as well as a sense of personal need.

If your group is fairly mature spiritually, you could follow this question up with: What role does Jesus play in our forgiveness (see 1 Jn 1:7-9)?

Question 6. Having been forgiven by God, David broke into a rhapsody of praise and strongly encouraged his people to pray to God and to find their security in him in troubling circumstances.

David addressed God personally as "you" (v. 6). He felt a sense of urgency about repentance and confession. Drawing on the commonly understood experience of training animals, he warned his people not to resist God's will or neglect his instruction (v. 9). David's release from guilt inspired him to urge others to rejoice in the Lord (v. 11).

Question 7. David found protection and a place of safety in God's presence and forgiveness. He sensed God's "songs of deliverance" (v. 7) around him.

He also knew God would direct his steps (v. 8) and surround him with his unfailing love (v. 10).

Question 8. A brief review is helpful. Take time to be sure everyone grapples with the big personal issues growing out of David's experience.

Question 9. People might want to reference the opening paragraph of the study on guilt that describes guilt as blame we have placed upon ourselves for something we did or thought, or did not do.

Question 10. This question encourages introspection about how each member is dealing with guilt and forgiveness. This may be difficult for some, but acknowledging how their path relates to David's experience can provide insight and healing.

Closing Prayer. Provide a time of silent prayer, followed by the opportunity for members to pray aloud.

Now or Later. For those interested in doing the "Now or Later" section on their own, you might explain that letters written do not have to be mailed; writing the letter can be healing in itself. Help members to see that writing about their thoughts can put guilt feelings into perspective and provide clarity.

Study 5. Sadness. Psalm 31.

Purpose: To face our sadness and discover how David turned to God when he suffered pain and loneliness in the wilderness.

Group Discussion. Many factors can contribute to sadness, such as loneliness, resentment, isolation, uncertainty, loss of control and depression. As members share their feelings, try to help them pinpoint what the greatest cause of their sadness is and when it occurs.

Question 1. Cover these word pictures quickly to establish David's walk with God, which was foundational to his gaining the help he needed.

Question 2. Among other things, David trusted God to save his life. When he said, "Into your hands I commit my spirit" (v. 5), he didn't mean he was about to die. Rather, it's a statement of his faith in God's strong love.

Question 3. Highlight the kind of relationship David must have had with God to describe his feelings so openly and graphically.

Giving people space to share openly about their own feelings (as David did) is key to healing.

Question 4. This question gets us in touch with human failing, even among those who claim to know God. David had certain expectations of his friends and neighbors that went unfulfilled. Help members share reasons why someone might have difficulty responding to a friend's loss or tragic circumstances.

Question 6. Help members be specific here as they look through the psalm. Nudge them to respond promptly and not overthink the question.

Question 8. This is an overall review question of the psalm.

Question 9. Come prepared with your own practical steps. How do you do it in your own life?

Question 10. Emphasize that reaching out to God and others is a choice. Choices like these can make a huge difference in our lives.

Closing Prayer. Confession can be done silently or out loud, depending on where your group is at.

Now or Later. There are many suggestions here for follow-up activities. You might want to read the suggestions aloud and ask for responses or questions about the ideas recommended.

Study 6. Hope. Psalm 33.

Purpose: To identify and engage in those aspects of life that can give us purpose and meaning, in order to move from despair to a hopeful future.

Group Discussion. This discussion is meant to remind group members of the things they value, and to help them start to reclaim the things that have meaning for them. This is important because as people lose their sense of purpose or meaning in life, it is very difficult to see any hope in the future.

Question 1. Music and singing were integral parts of Old Testament worship and praise of God.

Question 2. The focus on God is the key to worship and to finding hope in the midst of tough circumstances.

Question 3. A consideration of God's creation helps us to move from self-pity to thankfulness. Invite members to tell about their experiences with the striking beauty and power of nature.

Question 4. Political discussions are not appropriate. Point the discussion toward how the psalmist took a larger view and did not despair in his circumstances.

Question 5. Keep in mind that the basic purpose of this study is to get our minds off of ourselves and our sorrows and find hope in God's greatness.

Question 6. The psalmist begins with a call to praise as he finds hope in the reasons why God is worthy of our praise. In verses 18-19 he praises God because he is the certain protector of his people. He contrasts the uncertainty of human resources with God's care. "Death" (v. 19) refers to violent death by war, disease and famine. Famine was a common scourge in his time. He does not offer a false promise of protection from physical death. Jesus promised that those who believe in him shall never die, not physically, but spiritually. Christians find hope in his promise of eternal life.

Some in the group, however, may carry anger toward God. If anyone is honest enough to admit their anger, do not criticize or suppress them. They need to be assured of the group's acceptance and encouraged to express these feelings of anger toward God, who understands their pain.

Question 8. Aim for definitions in everyday language, not psychological answers.

Question 9. The psalmist's hope was based on God's character and power, not his own earthly desires. The idea of "vain hope" might be confusing. "Vain" could mean excessive pride, or something that's useless. Accept all ideas. Some may see hope as unattainable or useless. You might remind people that gaining hope is a process, not instantaneous.

Questions 10 and 11. Keep moving in your discussion and plan for plenty of time for these responses. You might want to circle back to the commands the psalmist issued (vv. 1-3).

Closing Prayer. Give time for members to pray silently. Invite anyone to offer thanks to God aloud before you end the prayer.

Study 7. Faith. Psalm 100.

Purpose: To help us move from doubt, disappointment or even anger toward a wholesome, healing trust in God.

Group Discussion. This week's opening question is a particularly personal one. You may find members in many different places in their faith walk. It is important for everyone to listen to each other without judgment, advice or preaching. Sensitivity is the key to this discussion. Invite members to talk about how they want to live and move from despair and hopelessness.

Question 1. Try to recapture the spirit of the occasion. Thousands would have gathered before the temple in Jerusalem, drawn by their desire to praise and worship God. Help the group imagine what was in the hearts and minds of those people as they celebrated and discern the psychological and spiritual value of joining in such corporate worship. Compare this kind of God-centered celebration with what often accompanies public demonstrations in honor of athletes, rock stars and politicians.

Question 2. For one thing, coming to Jerusalem to worship was probably costly for Jews, many of whom were poor farmers. Their faith also required the denunciation of false gods and renewed allegiance to Jehovah (v. 2 can be translated, "We belong to him" [TEV]).

Question 3. Allow time for personal thoughts to develop. Encourage honesty. By this time the members of your group should trust each other enough to admit how hard it is to have faith in times of loss and grief.

Question 4. The simple declaration "Know that the LORD is God" is the foundation of vital, life-changing faith. When we acknowledge we are God's, we take the first step toward healing.

In addition, faithful Israelites reveled in knowing God as their good shepherd (see Ps 23 for an example). Sheep, of course, occupied a prominent place in their lives, and the needs of their flocks were well known. The psalmist used a natural figure in a pastoral country. Sheep needed both water and pasture, which presented a daily challenge to shepherds in a hot, dry climate. Shepherds led their sheep to such places, while guarding them from dangerous paths and predators.

Question 5. Turning to the New Testament introduces a new and essential component of healing faith and trust. Resist the temptation to preach a little sermon here. Let group members think of the connections and illustrations from Jesus' life themselves.

Question 6. Encourage people to name as many illustrations from daily life as they can about what it means to be "the sheep of his pasture." Delve deeply into everything this covers in our lives.

Question 8. This isn't meant to shame those who don't attend church regularly. Rather, it's meant to highlight how valuable and healing corporate worship can be.

Question 9. After citing the reasons from the psalm, encourage discussion about how we move in our grief to see that God is good and loving. If you know someone in the group who is making progress in that direction, ask them to tell how it has come about in their experience.

Question 10. Review the main points of the psalm about who God is, how he relates to us, and how his love endures in spite of our pain, sorrow and loss.

Closing Prayer. Build in time for silent prayer. Then invite anyone who wants to to say a short prayer, perhaps a personal request to reveal his love and faithfulness.

Study 8. Acceptance. Psalm 37.

Purpose: To help us come to a place of acceptance regarding our loss and then grow in our knowledge of God's promises and care.

Group Discussion. Acceptance is not a one-time decision but a step-by-step process that takes time and patience. Encourage each person to share the beginning steps they are taking.

Question 1. David states his overall theme in verses 1-2, but see verses 1, 3-5, 7-8, 27, 34 and 37 for his specific exhortations. Take time to name each exhortation. You may even want to have someone write each one down as you move through the psalm. It might be hard for some people to only pick out the simple facts, but this is not the time to discuss each exhortation; just identify and clarify them.

"Dwell in the land" (v. 3) refers to God's presence with his people and the fact that he is their inheritance. True satisfaction is found in him. "Commit" (v. 5) includes the ideas of placing everything in God's hands, and giving our burdens and anxieties to him.

The second question here requires some thought, but it's important and valuable to get the big idea at the outset. Allow time and silence for quiet reflection. Then encourage people to interact with each other as they talk about their impressions of David's big idea. This is not a right-or-wrong, true-or-false question. Don't set someone straight who may think differently from others. David attacked the overall idea—"trust in the Lord"—from many different angles.

Question 2. David is so close to the Lord that reading his words can discourage us sometimes, because most of us are not on such familiar terms with God. But these traits were developed in him over time, not in an hour, a day or a year. He walked with God for many years—and he did, as we know, sometimes stray from the Lord too.

Question 5. Give people time to quietly reflect before answering. Thoughtful silence is extremely valuable.

Question 6. It's time to dig into the psalm again and look for specific promises. Ask someone to keep a list. Also, don't settle for religious jargon. Encourage down-to-earth responses. Another way to ask this is, "What does David say will be produced in us if we live out his exhortations?"

Question 7. Help people make the transition from what's in the Bible to their everyday life and experiences.

Question 8. This psalm, of course, demonstrates the ideal, but it helps to visualize the positive outcomes of accepting our grief and turning to the Lord for help, peace and guidance.

Question 9. This is the key practical question. We all need God's help in this matter. People in grief discover different paths to acceptance and wholeness. The Bible points us in the right direction through the examples of David and others. Looking at his psalm shows us that acceptance and praise are doable, even in the toughest experiences.

Questions 10 and 11. Watch your time as you go through the study so that you're able to get to these more personal questions.

Closing Prayer. After a time of silent prayer, invite members to thank God for the characteristics that make him so trustworthy.

Study 9. Praise. Psalm 71.

Purpose: To help us think about how to be thankful even while experiencing hard circumstances, and to appreciate the therapeutic value of praising God.

Question 1. This is the prayer of faith in the midst of danger. The psalmist took refuge in God and put himself under his protection.

Question 2. He emphasized God's righteousness; because of it, God did not abandon him. He was true to his word. He bent a listening ear (v. 2). God was his habitation, or stronghold, even in the midst of injustice and violence (v. 4).

Question 3. Notice his emphasis on hope, trust and praise, things he did even from his childhood and youth. His confession of faith moved others as well. Perhaps they thought his trials were punishment from God, but his faith remained unshaken.

Question 4. You could ask a few members in advance to tell their stories briefly here.

Question 5. The answer on paper is simple and clear, but difficult to practice.

Question 6. Invite people to share stories of successes and failures from their own lives—times when they were able to praise God and times when they tried to praise God but could not.

Question 7. This section begins with anguished prayers and ends with curses. Focus on the reasons for the psalmist's pain and his prayers.

Question 8. Vows, or promises, were taken much more seriously in the psalmist's time than in ours. Casting praise as a vow elevated it to the highest level of commitment to God.

The psalmist couples salvation with righteousness in verse 15 because the one is the outcome of the other; God's mercies are an inexhaustible theme.

Question 9. Whatever the psalmist's troubles were, they seemed like death to him. But he trusted God to bring him back from the (metaphorical) grave.

The words in verse 20, "though you have made me see troubles, many and bitter," may cause some to ask "Why *does* God allow evil and suffering?" This is a huge topic that cannot really be addressed here. Concentrate on the message in the remainder of verses 20-21.

Question 10. Praise was not an occasional act for the psalmist. He worshiped habitually, constantly. God's "wondrous works" (v. 17 kjv), that is, his power and love, are intended to arouse our praise, adoration, admiration and wonder. To celebrate God's deeds is both the duty and the delight of God's faithful people.

Closing Prayer. Make this a time of praise. Encourage brief prayers. Close the prayer time with a prayer of praise to God.

Now or Later. You may want to plan an activity together to honor the completion of the study. Because of the particularly personal nature of this guide, new friendships may have formed and deeper trust might have developed in your group. Celebrating this and giving members permission and an opportunity to have fun together can be very positive and reinforcing for the group, and is an important step in the healing process.

Appendix

The pain of loss and the process of healing can be overwhelming, and a very difficult path to walk alone. Without help and guidance, people often remain stuck in their pain, which can affect their entire lives. Having someone willing to walk with them through their pain and provide a listening ear can be a huge blessing. The extra help in this appendix will offer you ideas and tools to help you support those who are grieving and to facilitate a grief support group.

Tips for Starting a Grief Support Group

In starting a grief support group, there are some important things to consider:

- Find a quiet place to meet that will provide privacy for the group.
- Pray for God to bring members to your group.
- Be inclusive. Welcome people wrestling with all forms of loss: loss of a loved one, a marriage, a home, a job, etc.
- If possible, find a coleader to provide support.
- Plan for each session to be at least one-and-a-half to two hours. Allowing ample time for all to share in depth is important for a grief support group and critical to the healing process. And, in addition to the Bible study, there are components unique to a support group (such as having members share their personal stories and articulate how they're doing each week; see "The Important First Meeting" and "Subsequent Meetings," below) that you need to build in extra time for.
- Keep the size of the group small (six to eight members in the group, including leaders, is ideal). This will also facilitate sharing.
- Get creative in letting people know about the group. You might send out an invitation via letter or email, write up an announcement for your church bulletin, or enlist pulpit support, for example. Include your email address and phone number and/or the church office contact information so that those interested can sign up for the study or ask questions.
- Connect in some way with new members before the first meeting to become acquainted with the loss they are experiencing and to help them feel com-

fortable about attending. Making the decision to attend a group is often the hardest step for people in grief to take; this first connection is important.

- Call members before the first meeting to remind them about it. Forgetfulness is common when people are grieving.
- Read through the introduction to the leader's notes (pp. 44-48).

Tips for Leading a Grief Support Group

Those who are grieving a loss may be in an extremely fragile state, which means they might need an extra dose of love, care, gentleness and patience. These tips will help you as you walk this tender path of healing with the members of the group.

- *Listen, listen, listen.* Become an exceptional listener.
- Utilize the power of prayer in helping you prepare and in helping you be sensitive to the losses and sorrows within the group.
- Receive all answers warmly. Because members are dealing with painful losses, they need to be able to talk about their loss in a nonjudgmental environment.
- Be sensitive to the fact that members are traveling their own personal spiritual journeys. Some may not be believers and may have never opened a Bible. They may feel overwhelmed and intimidated when asked to find passages in the Bible, read aloud, pray aloud or offer answers to the questions. They also may not understand Christian terminology. Be prepared to offer gentle guidance and patience in these areas so that all feel comfortable and valued.
- Welcome tears and have plenty of tissues available.
- Bring extra Bibles to each session in case members forget theirs or do not have their own Bible. Also bring extra pencils, name tags and a dictionary. It's helpful to meet around a table.
- Consider providing some snacks such as nuts, crackers and water.
- Allow new people to come to the group through the first three meetings. Then close the group to new members in order to create an ongoing safe, trusting environment. (Allowing new people to join the group after the third session means time has to be spent reviewing each person's loss again and again. This limits the depth of sharing.)

The Important First Meeting

- Welcome all warmly. Introduce yourself and then invite the group to go around and each say their name. (They'll have an opportunity later to share more about themselves.)
- Invite each person to fill out and wear a name tag to help everyone remember names.

- Open with a brief prayer asking for God's blessing over the discussion.
- Explain your background and reasons for offering this grief support group. *Briefly* give your story.
- Pass out the LifeGuide booklets and review together "Suggestions for Individual Study" (pp. 5-6), which explains about the study itself, and "Suggestions for Members of a Group Study" (pp. 6-7), which covers important elements of positive group dynamics. These can be read aloud by the members of the group. Feel free to add comments regarding any guideline that you feel needs more explanation.
- Explain the importance of creating a warm, trusting environment so that all may feel safe. In particular:

  - Stress confidentiality. What is shared must be kept within the group.
  - Emphasize the importance of being great, nonjudgmental listeners.
  - Encourage members to offer supportive comments to one another at appropriate times, but also make it clear that they should not offer advice.
  - Explain the need for patience with silence and ask that the group not interrupt when someone is sharing or pausing to think. Pauses are often followed by deeper disclosures as members feel safe to share more of themselves and their circumstances.
  - Caution members not to offer platitudes such as, "It's a blessing that she's out of her misery," or "He is in a better place" (etc.). These comments, while thought to be helpful, can actually be quite painful.
  - Explain that tears are always welcome and that tissues will be available on the table, but ask the group to resist handing another person a tissue because that sometimes stops the person's sharing.
  - Encourage all in the group to share their thoughts and emotions, as this is imperative to the healing process.

- Review the timeline so that everyone understands how often the group will meet and the length of each session.
- Request that people contact you if they're going to be absent from a session so that the group will not experience worry or further feelings of loss. Be sure that all group members have your contact information.
- Ask if the group would appreciate a roster of phone numbers/emails/addresses so that they could have the opportunity to connect with and support one another outside of the meetings.
- Open the sharing with the following icebreaker: "Please share with us what loss you are experiencing and what you hope to get out of these sessions." Allow time for each person to share. This information will help the group to understand one another's loss and reason for attending. (The group can ask clarifying questions, but the primary goal is to listen to

one another. Also note that the time allotted for sharing will depend on the number of people in the group and the time frame of the meeting.)

- Do study one, "Denial."

  - At the end of the study, read the "Now or Later" suggestions. Ask the members to do the section on their own before the next meeting. Emphasize the healing value of these recommended activities. Some may wish to share (at the next session) what impacted them the most from doing the activities.

  - Encourage everyone to do study two before the next session to enhance the value of the lesson. However, also make it clear that they should still attend even if they cannot finish the lesson. (It is often very difficult for people in grief to read, study or even concentrate, so extra grace may be needed.)

Subsequent Meetings

- Starting with session two, begin all the rest of your group times by checking in with each person after the opening prayer. This "checking-in ice-breaker" is a vital part of a support group. Members will be more able to concentrate and learn from the study if they first have the opportunity to express their emotions and share significant events from the preceding week. This sharing also bonds the group and helps to foster understanding and empathy. You can simply ask something like, "Can you tell about what your week has been like and how you are feeling right now? And what impacted you the most from the 'Now or Later' suggestions in the previous lesson?" Allow time for all to share. (Again, the time allotted for this sharing will depend on the size of the group and the length of your agreed-upon group meeting time.) Then start in on the study for that week.

- If you do have new members at the second and third meetings, review "Suggestions for Members of a Group Study" again at those meetings, in order to ensure a safe, confidential environment. Also have any new members introduce themselves and explain what their loss is and what they're hoping to get from the meetings. Again, it is best not to add new members after the third meeting.

- At the end of the nine sessions, consider having the group plan an activity together. This can be a very encouraging way to honor the completion of the study. During the eighth or ninth session, take time for the group to discuss possible suggestions, dates and times for the activity.

Suggested Resources

Cutler, William, and Richard Peace. *Dealing with Grief and Loss*. Littleton, Colo.: Serendipity House, 1990.

DeVries, Robert C. *Getting to the Other Side of Grief: Overcoming the Loss of a Spouse*. Grand Rapids: Baker, 1998.

Elliot, Elisabeth. *Facing the Death of Someone You Love*. Westchester, Ill.: Good News Publishers, 2003.

Exley, Richard. *When You Lose Someone You Love*. Tulsa, Okla.: David C. Cook, 2009.

Faber, Rebecca. *A Mother's Grief Observed*. Wheaton, Ill.: Tyndale, 1997.

Haugk, Kenneth. *Journeying Through Grief*. 4 vols. St. Louis, Mo.: Stephen Ministries, 2004.

James, John W., and Russell Friedman. *The Grief Recovery Handbook*. New York: HarperCollins, 2009.

Kübler-Ross, Elizabeth. *On Death and Dying*. New York: MacMillan, 1969.

Lewis, C. S. *A Grief Observed*. New York: Seabury, 1961.

Mitsch, Raymond R., and Lynn Brookside. *Grieving the Loss of Someone You Love*. Ventura, Calif.: Regal, 1993.

Rainey, Barbara, and Rebecca Rainey Mutz. *A Symphony in the Dark*. Little Rock, Ark.: Family Life, 2009.

Staudacher, Carol. *A Time to Grieve: Meditations for Healing After the Death of a Loved One*. New York: HarperCollins, 1994.

Westburg, Granger E. *Good Grief: A Constructive Approach to the Problem of Loss*. Philadelphia: Fortress, 1971.

Cathy Gardner Maddams is a grief counselor and small group Bible study leader in San Jose, California. Jim Reapsome is a retired pastor, editor and writer in Downers Grove, Illinois.